Eagles
For Kids
Amazing Animal Books
For Young Readers

By Nicholas Williams
Mendon Cottage Books

JD-Biz Publishing

Read More Amazing Animal Books

Purchase at Amazon.com

Download Free Books!
http://MendonCottageBooks.com

Table of Contents

Introduction

Eagles are some of the largest birds of prey around – second only to vultures in terms of size – and are the ultimate apex predator of the avian (bird) kingdom. Feared by animals on land, sea, and even in the skies, eagles have developed a reputation for being one of the most lethal – and sometimes downright vicious – of wildlife species.

When most people think of eagles, they probably think of large fierce-looking birds with sharp elongated claws tearing apart some poor unfortunate rodent – and, unlike other wild animal stereotypes – it's actually pretty accurate. Eagles roam the skies high above most everything else and use their excellent vision to spot unassuming prey on the ground (or maybe in water – some species like to go fishing too).

Speaking of species, there are roughly sixty recognized eagle species (collectively known as the Accipitridae family) world-wide and they can be found on all the continents except Antarctica. The vast majority of them come from Europe, Asia, and Africa - but their worldwide presence has landed them on the coat of arms of many countries across the globe including Mexico in Central America, Egypt in Africa, and Germany, Poland, and Austria in Europe.

Throughout the rest of this book, we'll learn all kinds of interesting facts about some of the more popular eagle species and we'll explore their habitats, diets, lifestyle, mating, and more.

Habitat

We already mentioned in our introduction that at least one or more of the sixty or so known eagle species can be found on every continent except Antarctica. In spite of countless variations in the different species and the areas in which they live, there are some characteristics of their "living arrangements" that are shared across all the different eagle subspecies world-wide.

American Bald Eagle on Its Perch

Most of us are familiar with seeing eagles soaring across the sky – and maybe you've even seen one of them swoop down from above on some poor unsuspecting prey – but have you ever wondered where they live? Like many birds, eagles have nests, or perches, where they live, raise their young, and spend most of their time when not out hunting. Still, most people have never actually seen an eagle's nest – let alone one with anything in it – so you would be completely right to wonder where you could possibly find one.

Fortunately for the eagle, it makes its nest high above everything else that would ever go looking for it. Unlike most birds that make their nests on regular tree branches, eagles prefer to perch high up in the mountains and at the edges of the tallest cliffs they can find. They do, occasionally, perch in trees as well – but only in the tallest of trees that provide a maximum height advantage against potential threats (and prey) and only when sufficiently high alternatives are not readily available.

From its high perch, the eagle can have a bird's eye view of its surroundings – literally – even when at rest in its nest. They also have very good eyesight and this comes in very handy for keeping an eye out for a potential meal (like a mouse on the ground) or any potential threat. We can see that eagles are well adapted to life in the skies and their choice of home is perfectly suited to their position as apex predators and masters of their airborne domain.

Hunting and Diet

Eagles are birds of prey – which means they hunt down other animals as food. From their aerial vantage point, they can search the ground (or water) below for signs of a potential meal. A field mouse scurrying across a park is a likely target for a hungry eagle and opportune meals such as these are usually what brings these majestic birds close enough to ground level for the average person to get a good look at them. Unfortunately for curious bird watchers, eagles don't spend a lot of time close to the ground and, in fact, typically just grab their target and carry it back to their perch where they can eat and feed their young in comfort.

An eagle with a freshly caught fish.

The different eagle species across the world have widely varying diets. Some, like the Golden Eagle, have a diverse diet that consists of small mammals, fish, and other birds, while others have more specific diets such as the North American Bald Eagle that feeds almost exclusively on fish – though this may be more a matter of food availability than actual preference since fish are by far the most abundant food source for eagles in North America.

Eagles have a wide variety of similar, yet different, hunting methods. The hunt usually begins with the eagle soaring high above the ground scanning the terrain below for signs of food. Its excellent vision is critically important here since it allows the eagle to spot a target as small as a field mouse from many hundreds of feet away and slowly begin its approach – undetected by its hapless prey.

Once the eagle has located its target, it will approach its prey in a way that varies depending on many factors but, most importantly, the speed of the target animal and how likely it is to escape. Faster moving animals will most likely be attacked quickly and the eagle will descend rapidly upon the target before extending its feet and razor sharp talons to scoop the animal right up off the ground in one continuous – and very fast – motion.

Slower moving targets like turtles, as well as more dangerous targets like poisonous snakes, are be approached more slowly however. Slow moving prey are simply too easy to waste energy on swooping in on when the eagle can just cruise lower and lower and take its time as it approaches the animal that has little to no chance of escaping.

Dangerous prey on the other hand – especially poisonous prey that can mean death for the eagle with one well-placed bite – are approached more slowly for a different reason. Attacking such a potentially lethal target requires a cautious approach that allows the eagle to time its attack precisely to snatch the prey without being stung or bitten.

Finally, eagles also hunt other birds – often right out of the sky – and their primary targets are slow moving birds like geese and cranes. This is because eagles need either a speed advantage or an agility (maneuverability) advantage to successfully attack another bird in mid-flight. Faster birds will simply fly away before the it can attack and slower birds that are more agile will simply outmaneuver it until it gets tired and gives up.

An eagle's diet will, therefore, consist of whatever it can catch and bring back to its perch. This could be anything, really, but common prey includes:

- Fish

- Mice

- Foxes

- Snakes

- Other birds

Once the eagle has returned home with its catch, it will proceed to tear the prey apart with its sharp beak and talons.

Lifestyle and Mating

An eagle couple sitting together on a tree.

Eagles are very territorial and, in fact, territorial disputes are the reason for most conflicts between them. These disputes can turn into all-out fights and can even become fatal if neither bird is willing to back down.

Eagles that have reached maturity will seek out their own territory – usually in the same geographical area in which they were hatched – and claim it as their own by finding a suitable perch from which it can comfortably survey its surroundings. This helps it to detect, and respond swiftly to, any trespassers that might seek to harm it, or its territorial claim.

The young eagle will also be able to look out for potential meals – small mammals or fish perhaps – from the comfort of its perch. Readily available food actually appears to be the number one concern for eagles when selecting new territory to inhabit. Trespassing in another's territory in search of food can often lead to dangerous – though rarely fatal – confrontations.

Mating for most eagle species results in shared territory and is usually formed after an elaborate courtship display between the male and female suitors. These displays typically consist of a kind of acrobatic display of maneuverability and skill in mid-flight. For example, a male eagle might pick up a stone and carry it to a considerable height before dropping it – only to swoop down out of the air and catch it before it hits the ground. Female eagles often perform a similar display; but with something much lighter like a lump of clay.

Once a pair has mated, they stay together for life and some species like the Bald Eagle repeat the courtship display every year – possibly as a means of strengthening pair bonds. They may also engage in other activities like locking talons together and plummeting from the sky at high speed before releasing just in time to prevent collision with the ground.

As romantic as the parents might seem. life is pretty tough for an eagle chick. There are usually two eggs laid each mating season (though numbers as small as one and as large as four do happen). Whenever multiple eggs are laid, they are usually laid (and therefore hatch) days apart – which gives an obvious development advantage to offspring laid sooner rather than later. This becomes important when – almost inevitably – the "dominant" chick in the batch (usually the first-born and most-developed) kills its siblings right there in the nest under the watchful but indifferent eyes of its parents.

Some weeks later, the young eagle will be able to hunt its own food and, by the following year in most species, will have left its parents' territory to find one of its own. Later on, it will mate and raise young of its own and the cycle continues.

Some Popular Eagle Species

In this chapter, we'll look at some of the more well-known species and most interesting species found across the globe. From the temperate climate of North America, to the tropics of Sub-Saharan Africa, and even the frigid winters of Northern Scandinavia, we'll see the eagles that manage to thrive in all these different climates and learn how they've adapted to life in their unique environment.

Bald Eagles

Bald Eagle

The bald eagle is a very familiar sight to any proud American. As the national bird of the United States ,and also prominently featured on the

National Seal, the bald eagle enjoys a special kind of reverence among Americans that dates back to the foundation of the Republic in the 1700s when the seal was first adopted by the founding fathers.

Bald eagles live close to water and feed mostly on fish and, occasionally, aquatic birds. They build huge nests of up to 8 feet in width and 12 or 13 feet in depth. The largest bald eagle nests can weigh well over a metric ton! Definitely not something you'd want to be under when it falls so it's a good thing they build their nests at high altitudes – far away from people and other animals (except prey).

The bald eagle species has also flirted dangerously with extinction in the past and only very determined conservation efforts (as well as laws to protect them) allowed the bald eagle population to rebound from near extinction in the mid-twentieth century to a thriving population numbering in the hundreds of thousands across North America today.

Golden Eagle

The golden eagle is one of the most well-known birds of prey in the Northern Hemisphere. As one of the more voracious of eagle species, these natural-born hunters are exceptionally fast and wield thick, sharp, and lethal talons that enable it to kill even relatively large mammals like gray wolves.

Golden Eagle in Flight

In fact, the golden eagle has been historically popular for use in falconry – i.e. hunting wild animals using birds – and has been providing hunters with an aerial advantage over prey for centuries.

Crowned Eagle

The crowned eagle – also known as the African crowned eagle – is a powerful species that is indigenous and exclusive to Sub-Saharan Africa. It is widely regarded as the most powerful of birds of prey on the continent and as one of the most powerful land creatures on Earth (pound for pound). Attacks from this fearsome predator usually occur on the forest floor and involve various African monkeys, bush-bucks, and other mammalian species. The crushing force of its attack is often enough to kill its prey on contact and, if not, crowned eagles have been known to asphyxiate their prey quickly or to use their powerful appendages to crush them to death.

A Crowned Eagle.

One other hunting tactic that is somewhat unique to the crowned eagle is the "hunt-and-wait" attack. Sometimes, the eagle might be unable to immediately bring down a target animal and drag it back to its nest. This might be because the animal is too large to kill in a one-on-one attack , or perhaps because the animal is traveling in a group (as monkeys often do). In this case, the crowned eagle might stalk its prey for days until it seizes an opportune moment to strike its target quickly and fatally – though often not immediately. The eagle will then retreat to a safe distance and wait until its victim succumbs to its injury and can no longer keep up with its pack or fight back.

White-tailed Eagle

White Tailed Eagle Against A Sunset Sky

White-tailed eagles are very similar to the American bald eagles but live halfway across the world in Europe. Like its American counterpart, the European white-tailed eagles also face near-extinction before conservation efforts were put in place to save the species.

Their diet reflects the difference in location from their American counterparts, however. While the American bald eagles eat a diet mostly consisting of fish, European white-tailed eagles eat anything from lambs, to deer, to otters, and – of course – fish too. The increased variety means that White-tailed eagles benefit from being slightly larger than bald eagles since they have larger prey to hunt.

Fun Facts About Eagles

In this chapter, you'll find some interesting facts you probably didn't know about eagles (though at least one of them was mentioned earlier in this book – can you remember which one?).

- Bald eagles aren't actually bald. A very common misconception among people is that the famous bald eagle is completely bald and, therefore, has no feathers on its head. In fact, the bald eagle got its name from the color of the feathers on its head – white – and the illusion of baldness it appears to have created for whoever first coined the name.

- Bald eagles aren't born white-headed either. The next common misconception about bald eagles among people that know they actually aren't bald is that their heads are always white. In fact, bald eagles are born completely brown and it is only when they reach maturity that the feathers on their heads turn completely white.

- Eagles are found on the coat of arms of – not one – or even ten – but twenty-five countries world-wide! Not content with simply being an apex predator with no natural enemies, eagles have also proved their worth as symbols of strength, nationalism, and whatever else countries think about when designing their coat of arms.

- Golden eagles hunt larger prey than any of their peers – sometimes bringing down goats and even wildcats. When they attack and kill an animal that they can't carry back to their perch, they each eat their prey on the spot or make several trips back to their nest with manageable portions that they can carry. Makes for a pretty gruesome yet impressive dinner.

- Bald eagles can live for almost thirty years in the wild and up to 50 years in captivity! This puts them among the most resilient birds in the nature and makes them the longest living birds held in captivity

- Some eagle species pass on their nests to their children – sort of like an avian family inheritance. Homes being passed down many generations of up to 150 years have been recorded and trees in some parts of Scandinavia collapse regularly under the weight of very old eagle nests.

- The largest eagle on record was roughly nine feet wide (from wing-tip to wing-tip)! Many eagles are much larger than average humans – even if they don't seem that way from so far away as they fly overhead. Maybe it's a good thing they live in the remote mountain areas and on the edges of cliffs; far removed from civilization.

Conclusion

In this book, we've learned quite a bit about our apex predator friends in the sky. We've learned about where they live, how they hunt, and even how they socialize, and we've learned a few things about how use their natural talents to maximum advantage – an important lesson that we can apply to our own lives too. From their keen eyesight and ability to spot a potential meal from very far away to their sharp talons and powerful beaks used to tear apart their prey, eagles have developed into the ultimate predators raining chaos down from the sky on poor unsuspecting creatures.

We've also explored how eagle couples bond until death makes them part – something many people in committed relationships fail to do –

and this might teach us all something about loyalty. In fact, loyalty might be one of the traits that originally led even the rulers of the Ancient Roman Empire to hold this majestic bird in the highest regard. On the flip-side, we also saw a bit of the darker side of their nature when sibling rivalry gone awfully wrong leads to the untimely death of one or more chicks.

Finally, we talked a bit about some of the more popular eagle species around and learned a few fun facts about them that should help us appreciate them even more for the wonderful and marvelous creatures that they are while, hopefully, staying out of their way when they go hunting.

Author Bio

Nicholas Williams is a software developer, musician, and writer from Kingston, Jamaica. His passion for creating beautiful things that people can appreciate and enjoy permeates everything he does and he prides himself on his ability to use his talents to advance his own career while simultaneously expressing the diverse set of views he holds about life and the world we live in (with the hope of someday changing it for the better).

Horses
For Kids

Amazing Animal Books
For Young Readers
By John and
Annalee Davidson

Ponies
For Kids

Menlen Cottage Books

Amazing Animal Books
For Young Readers
Rachel Smith

Ten Amazing
Horses
For Kids

Nature Books for Kids
JD-Biz Publishing
K. Bennett

Akhal-Teke
"The Golden Horse
of the desert"
For Kids

Nature Books for Kids
JD-Biz Publishing
K. Bennett

Suffolk-Punch
"The Gentle Giant"
For Kids

Nature Books for Kids
JD-Biz Publishing
K. Bennett

Shires
"The great Horse"
For Kids

Nature Books for Kids
JD-Biz Publishing
K. Bennett

Colonial Spanish
"Horse of the Americas"
For Kids

Nature Books for Kids
JD-Biz Publishing
K. Bennett

Canadian
"The Little Iron Horse"
For Kids

Nature Books for Kids
JD-Biz Publishing
K. Bennett

Cleveland Bays
"History and Future"
Horses For Kids

Nature Books for Kids
JD-Biz Publishing
K. Bennett

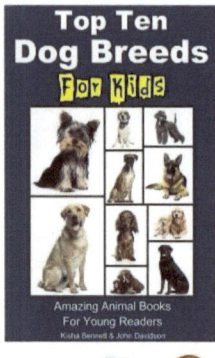

Top Ten Dog Breeds For Kids

Amazing Animal Books For Young Readers

Kisha Bennett & John Davidson

German Shepherds

Dog Books for Kids

K. Bennett

Bulldogs

Dog Books for Kids

K. Bennett

Dachshund

Dog Books for Kids

K. Bennett

Poodles

Dog Books for Kids

K. Bennett

Labrador Retrievers

Dog Books for Kids

K. Bennett

Rottweilers

Dog Books for Kids

K. Bennett

Boxers

Dog Books for Kids

K. Bennett

Golden Retrievers

Dog Books for Kids

K. Bennett

Puppies

Dog Books For Kids

Amazing Animal Books

By John Davidson

Beagles

Dog Books for Kids

K. Bennett

Yorkshire Terriers

Dog Books for Kids

K. Bennett

Dogs Top Ten Dog Breeds For Kids

Amazing Animal Books For Young Readers

Zahra Jazeel & John Davidson

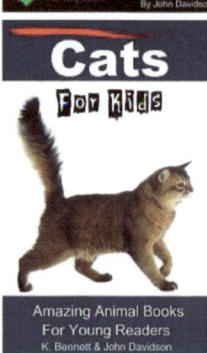

Cats For Kids

Amazing Animal Books For Young Readers

K. Bennett & John Davidson

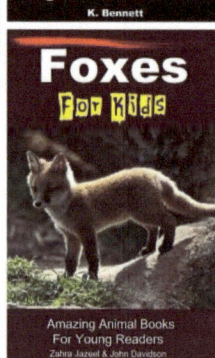

Foxes For Kids

Amazing Animal Books For Young Readers

Zahra Jazeel & John Davidson

Wolves For Kids

Amazing Animal Books For Young Readers

By John Davidson and Virginia Fidler

Our books are available at

1. Amazon.com

2. Barnes and Noble

3. Itunes

4. Kobo

5. Smashwords

6. Google Play Books

Download Free Books!
http://MendonCottageBooks.com

Publisher

JD-Biz Corp

P O Box 374

Mendon, Utah 84325

http://www.jd-biz.com/

Mendon Cottage Books

P O Box 374, Mendon Utah 84325

www.ingramcontent.com/pod-product-compliance
Lightning Source LLC
Chambersburg PA
CBHW050912290526

45792CB00002B/783